I'm Happy, Too?

I'm Happy, Too?

A Collection of Poems by: Renee Blackwell

Ignited Ink 717 LLC

Ignited Ink 717 LLC
Houston, TX

Cover Design: Ebony Rose of Ignited Ink 717 LLC

Categories: Poetry/Subjects and Themes/Death, Grief, and Loss; Self-Help/ Cutting & Self Harm

Renee Blackwell is available for performances, keynotes, panels, book talks, and workshops.

Discounts for bulk purchases of 25 books or more are available.
Visit IgnitedInk717.com or www.TheWrittenSociety.com to learn more and place an order.

For reprint permission, write to IgnitedInk717@gmail.com

ISBN (PRINT): 979-8-9991283-0-0

Printed in the United States of America

Dedication

For all of those whom I love and lost; and most
importantly those who came before me.

Foreword

Whooodaaawhooo are you ready? Are you sure? Proceed with caution.

The poetry you're about to experience is raw and poignant. If you're looking for apologies about the subject matter or the fiery expletives, you'll find them scattered amongst the ash. Sometimes, our ears have to burn to truly hear the truth.

Renee Blackwell, formerly known as Sad Renee, spares no flame and no gasoline in penning her latest release, *I'm Happy, Too?*, the highly anticipated follow-up to her first poetry collection, *I'm Happy*. Blackwell doesn't shy from taboo topics, her poetry explores themes such as depression, self-harm, self-loathing, and addiction.

I'm Happy was released during the peak of the pandemic, a time when the world was already in chaos. And yet, even then, Renee's words burned without permission.

But like many things birthed in survival mode, that collection deserved more. It deserved stillness.

It deserved celebration.

It deserved a second shot at being seen in all its complexity and courage.

I was initially apprehensive about asking Blackwell to revisit her scars. It felt selfish to ask her to return to the pain, the torment, and make art from it again.

I'm so glad she agreed.

I'm Happy, Too? is more than a rerelease.

It's a rebirth.

A smile rising from the ashes.

A chance to repackage the madness and make it beautiful again.

To hold space for the brilliance that flickers and to applaud the fire that roars. To honor a poet who refuses to water herself down. Not even a little.

As only Renee can, she took things further. She dove into her archives, dusted off notebooks, and found poems scribbled in the margins to give us a new experience—one that dares us to redefine what it means to be happy. One that dares us to find happy.

It has been a true pleasure creating with Renee over the years. Our paths are lit by the same flame. (Fun fact: we share a birthday— 7/17. There's *something* significant about that, though I'm not yet sure what.)

But I do know this: Where my voice whispers, Blackwell's echoes. Her boldness cannot be tamed. *I'm Happy, Too?* tore my heart to shreds, stitched it back together, and called it beautiful. Blackwell's poetry is a raging fire on paper. Prepare to be astonished and unable to avert your eyes. *I'm Happy, Too?* will captivate you, just like the inferno it is.

Preface

|

You should read "I'm Happy, Too?" with an open mind and heart. Do not rush. Take your time as you let the words resonate within your soul. At any time that you may feel overwhelmed, take a break, and breathe. This book is a part of my growing pains. These pages host the resurrection of my poetry, of my healing, and of my smile.

How has your journey been since you originally released *I'm Happy* in 2020?

My journey since publishing my first anthology has been an emotional roller coaster. I began with optimism, certain that I would become a best seller. But there were moments when I hated my book —times I couldn't even bear to look at it because it felt like a symbol of my failure.

And yet, I would do it all over again, without hesitation. My book is my legacy, a testament to my existence. Somewhere in the world, someone understands me because of it. I've accomplished something I once thought was impossible.

This book—my baby—has placed me in a constant state of vulnerability. Reading it is like looking into a mirror and confronting the versions of myself I've hidden away just to survive. When I feel unbearably isolated and consumed by my emotions, I turn to my book for comfort. But I also read it to challenge myself, to confront the parts of me that still haven't healed.

THE CONTENT

RENEE BLACKWELL

Letter to My Vices

|

Do you remember when we first met? The first time that I sought you out for comfort? How do you feel when you see me cry? And when I reach out to you with a broken heart, does that break you? Or are you just an enabler? What would we be without each other? If I chose to feel the pain over my preference for the numbness that I seek, who would I be? Would I survive? Do you resent me as much as I resent you? Do you love me as much as I love you? Do you pity me? Do you profit from my pain? Or are you the prophet of my pain? The only way for me to get the answers that I need is to try , but what if I don't want to? Or worse, what if I don't like the person that I am without you?

Heel to Sole

|

Do you love me?

A question that I ask more than I care to admit

Yet, I hear the answer loud through the whistles and wind

A freight train

You could never deliver what I needed the most.

Full speed you ran and never stopped

Heel to sole

The arch in your feet aching

knowing that I was suffocating

but you never cared to breathe life into me

Heel to sole

Permanent indents in the fabric that was supposed

to protect

Me.

Us.

The materialistic veil shedding to pieces as you

continued to run

Body in perfect form

It's the only thing you could do well

Head high

Confidence glistens on your skin

No shame as you'd run past unpaid balances

And broken promises

And me

broken

You're the fastest, my love, how do you run so well?

Who taught you to cower?

Who taught you to sacrifice my heart for the sake of your own selfish vices?

Who taught you to be afraid, alone, insecure and unsure?

Who can I blame?

Heel to sole

I run as well

Not behind you

But beside you
Because I'm afraid that if I pass you that would be the end of us.

Heel to sole

I ache

Ligaments, don't fail me now.

The obsession to prove myself worthy of you consumes
us both.

Do you love me?

The answer loud and clear

As your footsteps keep the same pace matching my
anxious heart

Heel to sole

This marathon is eerie

There's no one on the sidelines cheering me on

Just you watching me disintegrate

With no way to heal the soul.

Chaos Queen

|

There's a charm in the volatile grip of chaos.

I can't quite explain how kinetic it is,

but it's alluring.

It pulls you in

you aren't able to escape.

It's not like you'd want to anyway

The flames feel too much like home

smoke signals in my handwriting

That best friend you're all too familiar with

four-page letters riddled with secrets,

and repeated lyrics laced with lullabies

You are chaotic

and messy,

and trouble.

You stir up feelings

spinning those unfortunate enough

to be within your proximity

You are a hurricane of lust and passion.

You are moans and broken breaths.

You suffocate your lover.

You apply pressure to their throats.

Tears of pain

only superseded by the flowing rivers of pleasure

that roar beneath your feet, Poseidon.

Yes, there is undeniable beauty in chaos

I see the dysfunction and it turns me on.

It turns me into this person

that I see but I can't touch.

Chaos.

Turmoil.

Toxicity.

The adrenaline that rushes to my head like my favorite

drug; not of choice but of need.

Second nature.

The force that drives me to live.

What a beautiful thing.

My Familiar

|

I know that we were lovers before.

I've fallen for you many times in our past lives.

I can feel it each time that I kiss you.

When you take my face in the palm of your

hands

We've done this before.

Me fighting the injustices of this world

speaking out for the voiceless.

When my tongue was stolen from its home,

you were there to remind me in each life

of how strong I was.

Just like you do now.

This whirlwind romance isn't as spontaneous

as we think

this cyclone has consumed us before...

remnants of our remembrance

still exist between its gusts

waiting to be blown away into yesterday

You've laid my body on the altar

ancient symbols etched into our hearts

Our soprano notes envied by the gods

echoing into eons of the night.

I've taken your hand hundreds of times

and placed it on my heart

your fingerprints branded into my flesh

throughout all the times

that I've been reincarnated.

I'm sure I've written these words before.

Maybe with an ink-stained feather.

Maybe with a mixture of our blood

as I drank and drank.

From a bottomless bottle of hope

pouring glass after glass

of emptiness and we became one.

I wish that I could tap into the consciousness

that would allow me to remember

every detail of our love.

I wish I knew how our story ends

...this time.

Young Lady

|

I watched you try to break me

You told me with awe mixed with admiration

and a slight tone of humor,

I was tough.

You cupped my chin brought my eyes

to meet yours.

And all I could think of was,

What a menacing smile you wore

It was maddening.

Quite hypnotic

I felt so undignified and bare.

You put me on this vast stage

An attentive audience of one

Performing at beck and call

I hated it

Or perhaps I hated how much I loved it.

Memories kept safe, in my deepest part

peaking out without permission,

disregarding boundaries,

definitely a reminder of you

Everlasting shame

as I run my hand over my bruised skin

hot and cold

Plumply swollen

I watched how you took care of me

as well as you destroyed me.

Your affectionate embrace

as aggressive as your hand pushing my head

to please you down below.

This was an all-new high and low

Interchanging,

fluid as anyone's sexuality can be

I am able to break out of my cocoon

and fly

Wind whipping across my skin

like the paddle across my bare ass.

This is the moment where I realize

I can not be broken.

I am free.

I am empowered.

I am under the notion

that I am giving away control

but you let it be known

that it is I

who controls you.

I moan out in pain

and my eyes become as wet as my yoni

I have one of the most gratifying orgasms

that anyone could be blessed with.

I crave the kiss that changed our dynamics.

Filled with passion and yearning

We were no longer preying on each other

We were no longer on the hunt to kill

To fulfill our lustful and filthy inhibitions.

I'll forever be.

Yours truly, Young Lady.

Weight Room

|

Sliding over wet words

transforms lust into poetry

Feelings stutter, hung on hesitation

may never come out.

Eyes focused- tuned into another dimension

only you and I exist.

Shooting lasers through walls.

Crumbled sheets

Battered pillows.

I give all my weight to you.

Chance

|

I smell

the sweetest scent.

I taste

your love on my tongue.

I feel you

And before I get a chance to react.

Chance reacts to me.

Confinement

|

4 walls closing in

I am not able to breathe
for fear that the walls will suffocate me

Pushing me to my limits

Choking on trust

I yell for help to no avail

This space is too small
This love is too vast

My heart is too weak

Broken since birth

I never experienced her love

I was never allowed to laugh and play

No fresh air. No grass

Itchy and lovely

No bugs to crawl on my legs the same way his hands

did

This life is 4 walls

Closing in

I can not escape

I can not breath

for fear that all of my triggers

Will suffocate me

I became its prey as it pounces with intensity

My mind has never been allowed to explore until
now

When confinement is only a figment of my disorder
Swallow the pills
and they all disappear to another room
with 4 walls

Weeping Hollow

|

Why don't you cry?

Little rivers flowing from shallow holes

Dripping downward dissipating

Why won't you weep?

Echoes of a heartbeat decelerating

I'm just trying to understand

Why can't you sob?

Are you that traumatized?

Are you that numb?

Why are you such a monstrosity?

Crying will humanize you, love.

Don't be afraid to wail.

Don't be afraid to let go.

You should scream...

Until you have no voice!

Until you have no choice.

Until no one can hear you cry.

That voice that's never heard.

"Little meek girl. You're a weak girl. Because you weep."

Lessons

I was never taught how to be a daughter

How to take advice from an elder

I was never taught to listen

To sit still while reality moved around me

Fast paced little ants scurrying to the hill

Their castle, their fortress

I was never taught to love

and to accept things as random

No one ever cared enough to teach me how to fly

I did learn to imagine

To concoct stories so elaborate

that even I may have believed them

I learned to be skittish and independent

I learned to hate myself and everyone around me.

No one taught me.

The Artist's Burden

|

The artist holds the key to other realms.

It must be such a heavy but exhilarating burden
to carry.

In what other ways can you explain the
complexities of their mind?

The artist can not be stuffed into a box
shipped to convenience, routine, and lackluster.

They must be bubble wrapped, tightly bound
because without them we live in a dull world.

A passionless world, where emptiness

is just emptiness and there's no way to write it out,

sing at the top of your lungs,

or let your hands take control

as they move with intent to create magic.

I long for the moment where I am able to create

a masterpiece out of pure happiness

instead of tragedy,

but perhaps it is the price that I pay.

Sentenced to live a life of torment, constantly haunted

by my demons.

Driven to the point of insanity only to be pulled over

and arrested by my art.

There's always a fine to pay.

Someone has to suffer to ease the sufferings

of their fellows.

The Most High

|

How many times must you get high before you realize ,
you're miserable?

Hurting others because you fail to feel,
because you can't seem to heal.

Hurting others because you are ignorant
of the fact that love can be pure.

Truly unadulterated
But darling,
You don't believe that.

How many hits does it take for you to leave?

Drop that baggage off at the dumpster
it's no use to you.

You're convinced that you are nothing
you don't deserve all the goodness
that the great gods could send you

How could you forsake me?
The Gods of Adornment Bliss
Will I find my beloved?
Do I know how to love?
Why is my love of choice broken?
And sad?
And high?
Questions that need answers.

Hungry

|

Starved and deprived

I hear the sound of my heart fading away

My knees bloody and bruised

Voice sore from repeating the same phrase

from hours on end, *Thank you, Jesus*

I eat the words with hopes of fulfillment

Hungry for faith ,Love, FOOD

the nourishment that a body needs to grow strong

bones and mind

My chest heaves violently

Crying Hard

Not because I am moved by the spirit

but because I am hungry

Hallucinations become my reality, *Who is that man?*

That pale literary figure sitting on his throne

Watching me starve AND pray

But he was real. I saw him.

Instead of seeing myself

That was the highest honor,

To replace myself with God

Yet, I was still hungry

Alone in psychosis

With the bible and my journal.

Starved.

Undress in Black

|

I go home and undress

somehow my sadness still clothes me

It covers me even after I've ripped off my bra

and untangled myself out of the thongs

that grip me.

It still lingers.

Even after I've wiped off my mascara and eyeliner

It's chronic reoccurring.

My best friend.

I've learned to count on it to be there when my lovers

fail me.

My moods have imprisoned me

I've pushed away everyone

But they were never really there

I never let them in.

I apologize for my sadness,

it's selfish and wants me all to itself.

And by god trust me

I've tried to break it off

I've courted true happiness, it was all too fake.

Ingenious smiles and laughter.

I've slid in the dms of breathing

because you know they say it helps.

Every time I inhale anxiety attacks

and sadness rides my exhale

Rejected by the simplicity of life's offerings

How am I still alive?

What is my purpose?

When will I feel the warm embrace of happiness

within?

Do I even want to?

Am I that co-dependent to the suppression and

repression that relies heavily on me?

Muscle Weight

|

Weightless in the air

I fly freely within myself

My wings beat against the wind

just as the violence I'd become accustomed to

Wet towels whipping against my back

Pray LOUDER

Drifting off to sleep

I pray to deaf ears

Floating on clouds

Ears popping

Turbulence be still no more

Help

Weightless in my sorrow

My woes buried deep in smiles and dancing

Resentment must fill the heart of my existence

Standing in concrete

Hand raised to the ceiling

That's as high as my dreams went.

No further than my near sighted vision allowed me

to see

Praying to a savior for my savior

with bruised lips

Where is my father?

I need my mother.

My sister has disappeared

My sister hurts more than I do

Does she love me?

Does the abuse haunt her in her slumber

as it haunts me in mine

Does she get so hungry that she'd rather starve?

What does she believe in and

does she believe in me?

Does she believe like I believe in ancestors that we

only share half of?

That she would never acknowledge.

Did she find herself in wine and time?

Time.

Hasn't healed my wounds

Exposed

Like my mother

Did she sell her dreams in hopes that her pain

would subside?

Maybe we're all weightless

Floating around each other

Not really existing

Ghosts of our newborn state

May they live in peace.

May I rest, weightless in chaos

My grave unvisited

as I lived

Barely loved.

Sad Mistress

|

Excuse me, my love.

Forgive me, but I need to be alone with my mistress.

What?

Don't act like you didn't know.

Wake up!

Why would I realize you're my dream?

Should I give it all up for you?

I'm sorry, my love,

but my mistress isn't really my mistress

She was here before you

I'm sure we'll share coffins

our bones kissing under the same tombstone

She's constant

all I have to do is give her access to my heart.

She pleases me in ways you couldn't imagine

I need her more than you.

She fills voids you couldn't reach

I feel bare without her

I keep her close to the flesh

Forgive me, my love, but you could never compare to

her

She is my sadness

and she means everything to me.

Surrounding me

controlling like anxiety

I'm getting found in insanity

I can sleep well

because she puts me to bed without much effort

Her embrace has that effect on me.

She has a way of making me feel everything

but nothing at the same time.

She brings me gifts

wrapped with a false sense of security

I have no choice but to accept it with a smile.

The bow promising brutality if I decide to decline.

I could do without the comfort of heartbreak

and heartache.

I'm not sure that I want to.

She's constant.

She's reliable

When everyone else leaves she's rooted there.

In my heart.

My soul.

So forgive me, my love, if I can't seem to cheer up.

She owns me.

I belong to her, not you.

Functionally Depressed

|

There is an internal struggle

that seems like it's eternal.

You crave to have normal feelings.

You're numb majority of the time

but when you feel it's like a tsunami.

Sitting at your work desk, functioning while depressed

in group chats filled with 'lol's

you've never really had

Dancing at your favorite bar belting out drunken

karaoke all while depressed.

Blushes and touches

Tangled tongues

Pants and moans

All while fucking depressed!

How depressing is that?

Now tell me how strong I am.

How I am still here and I'm a 'survivor'

But the only thing I'm 'surviving'

is another painful day

The only thing I've 'survived' is the booming solitude

that I reside in everyday

So tell me how I'm a modern-day heroine.

How I've saved the same hoes

Who I loved who never really loved me.

They never saw that dark shadow looming over me

They never tried to seek out the hidden identity

that self-loathed and self-doubted

They didn't bother to intercept my telepathic messages

I am hurting.

I don't want to live.

And still,

I get applause and congratulations

Are the pieces of confetti

to commemorate every pill I took...

or thought about taking?

Are the bouncy balloons

for the days I wanted to float away

...never to return? A memory in the clouds.

Cutting the cake

just as precise as when I cut my wrist .

Licking the icing and savoring the moment.

Do you understand now?

How preposterous this celebration is?

There's nothing celebratory

about how I could slit my wrist right now

and be at peace.

AND STILL, BE EVERYONE'S PEACE.

And a best friend.

And a lover.

And an aunt.

And an entrepreneur.

All while

I'm depressed.

Citrus

|

Whispers of sun rays softly brush my face

With my head titled back and lips slightly parted

I accept this intimacy

I crave it, really.

Because Sunshine tastes like love

Even when the clouds are soft and dark

I still fill the black hole and emptiness that love brings

to me.

Who am I without it, after all?

Sunshine tastes like her

A shadow looming over my heart

Sweet and savory, her kisses cut like knives

I love sharp objects

I've become accustomed to burning myself

And healing myself just to prove that no one else can

take care of me like I can

Because sunshine tastes like mangoes

I rip through the flesh with my teeth

Letting the juices flow down my chin

Sunshine tastes like her

Or perhaps it tastes like Louisiana

The sweaty air still hangs on my tongue.

I'll never get that freedom I felt as my body rolled

down the hill.

Laughter, bugs, and traffic became my soundtrack.

Memories are memories, whether painful or endearing.

I've tasted sunshine, rain and snow.

I've tasted blood, tears and sweat.

I've tasted life and kissed death.

Above all, sunshine is internal and eternal.

Sunshine is consistency.

A new day to get life right.

It absolutely, undeniably tastes like that moment when you start to grieve.

Sunshine tastes like my mother.

Originally published in Ignite-Her by Ignited Ink 717 (2025).

Freedom

Freedom feels like a soft kiss after I've been hit

Punched in the gut

Vomit spilling onto my shoes

Love is hard

And painful

But I endure it

I deserve it

The punch and the kiss.

Cat Scratch

|

I know you won't believe me

but the scars on my arms are from my cat.

The cat that I nurture and love

scratches and bites the shit out of me

And because I learned at a young age that love is pain

I continue to love and nurture him.

See, he is my child and it's funny how this is a recurring

theme in my life.

I am drawn to things that I know have the potential

to harm me.

The truth is that I love danger and historically have
no regard for my life.

I can't lie and say that, when I saw the river of blood
mapping its way down my wrist that I wasn't tempted
to create the most beautiful and self-deprecating art.

The need to make the cut a little deeper
and bleed a little more stirred up old feelings.

The voices screamed at me through the blood

You can not run from me.

I will always be here.

My cat scratched the shit out of me and I realized that I was not healed.

I am a fraud because I preach growth, love, mental health awareness and self -love, but in that moment all I wanted to do was feel my flesh split into a two way street of self-hate and escapism.

I wanted to feel the rush as I watched each drop of blood spill onto my hardwood floors.

A testament that I could never escape my trauma.

And so I imagined that I gave in to those old feelings waking up in a small pool of my own blood.

Dried, crusted blood

on whatever body part I blessed.

Thighs

Arms.

Legs.

Stomach.

There was no shame back then,

but when my cat scratched me

and I felt the thirst to self mutilate I felt ashamed.

Is that growth or cowardice?

APB

|

I need to put out an APB
The hour hand has swung around
too many times since I've seen her.
Time doesn't fight fair.

She was last seen wearing a smile.
The kind birthed from a good thing.
Rose quartz and amethyst in her steps.
Manifesting love wherever she went.

Her last declaration digging in my ear
'I'm Happy'
Deeper

'I'm Happy'!

Deeper

'I'm Happy!!'

Deeper

Til I pay in blood.

You found her?

Are you sure that's her?

She's different.

Her blossoming breaths

are now a dead bouquet in a shallow grave.

This shell can't be her.

Hollow and dark.

Where has her light gone?

Who can rekindle her joy?

I look at her

staring back at me .

Hollow holes full of despair

I don't know where to begin.

'Where Am I?'

My Existence: evaporated into memory

This empty must be what black holes are made of

Galaxies swallowed whole

Civilizations: crtl + alt + deleted

All tasks ended

Evidence

Void of validity or relevance

No trail to discover, Myself

Where have I gone?

Where have I gone?

No traces in the spaces between the lines

criss crossed in my mind

Fear held my heart.

Tying knots with each vessel.

Fashioning it to its ring finger

Vowing to be a present partner

No matter which end of the spectrum circumstances

were gifted from

Giving me something to have and to hold

I welcome it to slip through my fingers

I've loosened my grip on everything else

You are not exempt

It's quiet I freeze

when numbness starts to set in

I just want to feel....Happy

I just want to fill...Me.

Again.

Creation

|

I wonder if you know how perfect you are?

You're a wicked kind of extraterrestrial.

Your aura...stains my life...

a trail of blood leading to euphoric escapades

I cling to the notion that I could one day be as willing

and open...And ready...

And bloody humble as you are.

But I am an egotistical, maniacal fool

who believes that I, too, could be perfect.

You're an aesthetic

You're the top row on the explore page.

An icon.

You stride effortlessly and I don't envy that.

I feel pity because you are at your peak

and I haven't peaked yet

so yea, there's hope for me, but that's it for you

I've murdered you a billion times

just to resurrect you,

because I haven't found the perfect death for you...

yet

It should match your ferocity and passion.

It should be pristine and filthy.

Your death should be celebrated held in high esteem

digging the grave for all other deaths to come.

I may be fighting a losing battle with this silly

notion, but I must try.

Your strength is a mood and your love is a vibe.

I know that we are one and the same,

but my mind doesn't comprehend simple thoughts.

Gaze of The Guardian too abstract

to see that you and I are both wonders

of this world.

Who knew the 8th would be a towering 4'11

a spectacle with specs Two faces guarding the same

purpose

We are creation

Golds

|

I just want to be beautiful.

Breathtakingly beautiful.

The perfect sunset, All back-lit and shit

Golden, flakes of greatness peeking from within

Nefertiti skin

shimmers so Queenly

I want to feel beautiful.

Insanely beautiful.

The wind that whispers tales

of happily ever after on your cheeks

on a magical summer day

Beautiful like the smell of home.

Beautiful like ,"let me be of help to someone today"

Beautiful like Maya Angelou's poems.

Beautiful like the Orishas' embrace.

Magic

I want to be magical af

I want to possess that kind of magic

that loves everyone.

That shit is beautiful!

That's what I strive to be,

because right now and as long as I can remember

I've always been ugly.

That self-loathing kind of ugliness

That ugliness that goes from being

your shadow to being your soul.

It's a part of you

the only way to kill it

is to kill yourself,

but you can't

Or you won't?

because you're afraid of what will be left.

Full of emptiness- yet fulfilling.

I wish to be beautiful.

I wish to be someone who smiles

and actually means it.

I'd give anything to be anyone in this vast world

I don't ask for a big ass, a small stomach,

and a full bosom

I just want to be beautiful.

I just want to be the definition of love.

Write Happy

|

This is my attempt to write happy

to find favor and beauty in the world

in which I reside.

Pure beauty

Not the ugly kind of beauty.

Or the Haunting kind of beauty

Nor the Beauty that brings about pain.

Classic beauty.

Like a sunflower basking in a daze of sun rays,

lips spread like petals, heaven behind sunshades

Air blowing through my hair

as I sing and dance along to the rhythm

of liberation

A genuine laugh that comes from deep within.

The kind of smile that fits perfectly on my face.

This is my attempt to find beauty within myself.

Not the ugly kind of beauty.

Or the haunting kind of beauty

Nor the Beauty that brings about pain.

Classic beauty.

To feel worthy of compliments

To receive praise without blushing with frustration

Like a Sunday morning, I give thanks to you, Oshun

My mirror... on my bleeding knees ...

a blessing Ase'

Please allow my ears and heart to hear

simple truths that sound like,

'You are beautiful inside just as much as you are

outside',

'Your aura is captivating and your energy is

hypnotizing and intoxicating',

'You are capable of true love

because

you ARE

true

love',

'You are strong', 'Your crown is fit for a crown',

'You are worthy' and 'You're perfectly you'.

This is my attempt to let myself know

that there is beauty without pain.

How'd I do, you?

Rituals

|

All we do is cheat each other and share love songs.

It's silly.

You and I together

are chaos and dysfunction

but we always find time for our rituals

We release 'I love you', 'I'm sorry' and 'I forgive you'

into the universe and it becomes a boomerang

of insanity.

When will we realize

we will never be a great love story?

You have infatuation.

I have nothing.

So we send love songs full of nostalgic lyrics

from when we were our worst selves.

Back when I craved attention and you craved me.

I intentionally put you under a spell.

I bounded us together

I needed you as a constant

in the midst of my instability.

You always come back to me

and I always come for you.

You consistently said that my pussy belongs to you

and I responded by rolling my eyes

but in hindsight it may be true

because that's all that I can offer you.

So we perform our rituals.

Seeking out each other's bodies

eventually falling into a fallacy

Delusional dancing to the tune of 'My First Love'

Look at the mess of us.

You're unattainable.

I am unavailable.

As we blush on the couch of truth and lies.

So tell me my lion, what are we doing?

Will we become stars of the black swan?

We perform our rituals.

Synchronized.

Hypnotized.

Desensitized.

All over and over and over and over again.

We intensely try to create the magic

we wish that we could have together.

Look at us now - still chaotic, but beautiful.

Bruised but still willing to love through resistance.

You - gentle but impenetrable.

Me- crazy but somehow the sanest of the both of us.

We perform our rituals.

We perform our rituals.

We perform our rituals.

Until we have nothing left to believe in.

Short Lines from Poems that I Never Finished

|

1

Death could be an endless sleep or a new life, but it
couldn't be hell, for I know torment.

2

My love can be obsessive

Addicting.

Toxic

But I'm convinced that you prefer your love

that way.

3

Penetrating your mental. Words overflowing from
your mouth like a fountain of praise in the form of
moans.

4

We came together.

Party of two.

5

She found sanctity in my heart. Home in my embrace and power in my yoni.

6

Your love feels like snow in Houston.

Rare and cold.

7

In English we say, 'You've broken my heart'.

But in poetry we say , 'Death by a billion cuts pales in comparison to the ache that you've brought upon me.'

How does it feel to hold such power?

To send me out to battle with a dull sword

My Spoken Words

|

Once I found my voice, I started using it. Literally.
These are poems that leaped off of the page onto
the stage.

|

An Ode to the Weird Black Girl

|

I see you struggling, Sis.

I can tell that you feel out of place

Like you have no space.

But, Sis.

Listen.

You don't rank in the top 5, because you're are the

1%.

They don't understand how you can wear your pain

like red bottoms.

They don't understand why you cloak yourself in black
and headbang like you invented that shit.

Cause you invented that shit.

Never forget that shit.

Sis,
I know you hear the laughs when you rock your fro
and they call you a nappy headed ho,
but that don't have shit to do with you.
They don't understand how grounded you are.

They don't hear the friction when your nappy ass
fro sway from side to side
and you hear your ancestors say
"I got you"

They don't have antennas like you, so they can't experience life like you.

Sis, I know that they call you weird.

I know that you feel like an alien but perhaps it's because you're an ethereal being who surpasses boundaries and bleeds creativity.

They lust after your aesthetic on Instagram,but bash you in reality.

Their 3rd eye isn't activated so they can't see what you see.

My point is, Sis, hold your head high.

There are people who were meant to follow the societal rules, but clearly that's not you.

You beautiful black, wide nosed, big lipped, wide hipped, chocolate dipped, locced hair, funky dressing, head scarf wearing, "ghetto" name having, crystal collecting, yoga addicted, meditating, vegan, Scifi and anime loving, cosplaying, sun bathing, daydreaming, poetic, intelligent, insistent, consistent, passionate, self loving, gothic, waist beads adorning, artistic goddess.

You are everything that one can inspire to be.

Be that, Sis.

FYRP

|

Censoring my art is like telling me I can't play with
my pussy

How dare you try to pass my pride off as tawdry

Am I measured in orgasms or degrees

Or the lack thereof?

Censoring my art is like prohibiting a mother from
breastfeeding in public.

It's asking me what I was wearing when I was
raped. Was I flirty? Was I drunk?

It's undignified.

Immoral.

It's denying me a job because my skin is too dark and my hair is too nappy.

As if I'm not proud to be too black and too damn nappy

It's calling my cornrows boxer braids.

Because the braids that fashioned by black women aren't high fashion until some pale chick with a BBL and lip injections wears it on the gram

As if AAVE ain't poetic as fuck

Like my poems that may be too much

Sadness

But,

fuck!

I can't put out no watered down shit to pacify the

masses.

My art can't be censored.

And when I say fuck your

respectability politics I really mean that shit

like when I say

Fuck my abuser

Fuck my ex - that motherfucker never deserved me

anyway

Fuck racism and homophobia

Fuck the government

Fuck the elitist and classist

Fuck George Zimmerman

Fuck my job

Fuck your bitch and the clique you claim

Fuck everyone who ever wished for my downfall
and

Fuck you.

You who wish to censor my art.

I bleed these words as they flow out of my uterus

and I allow them to free fall running down my legs

spilling onto the floor staining my world of earth

tones and black .

My art looks quite violent and yet

I collect my menses and wave the red flag.

Vulnerable. Exposed.

I do this because I have to.

I'm in too deep in this life so it's write or die.

My art can't be censored.

Bitches ain't been shit but hoes and tricks since 1992 but it's a problem now that the Girls are limiting their dating pool to men with means and wealth and good dick

Fuck the patriarchy

I deserve to be blatantly sexual
My appetite shouldn't be held hostage to the four walls
that tell no tales

And really

Shouldn't beauty be shared and celebrated

Shouldn't art be filled with passion

I'm not ashamed to say that my art is

uncomfortable

Honest

Chaotic

because Ima profane bitch

who uses profane words

Bitch

Ho

Suck my proverbial dick

It's sick how my colorful language is more offensive

than how our basic human rights are being stripped

away.

Snactched from our arms like my innocence was
snactched from me.

Still he mansplains to me and say that true artist can
get their message across without using every curse
word in the book

So let me say this in a way to appease his false sense of
superiority

I, Renee Blackwell will not adhere to society's
benighted expectations of socially acceptable behavior.
I respectfully decline your invitation.
My art is nonnegotiable.

In other words

bitch

fuck you

my art will not and can not be censored

My breast will not be censored .

My hips will not be censored.

My laugh will not be censored.

My art is the true definition of a woman.

Relentless.

Dangerous.

Intimidating.

Godly.

Censored.

My art is black as midnight

garnished with the whispers of my ancestors.

It's freedom, but how can I truly believe I'm free if

every word I say is being censored?

If how I choose to love my lover out loud is being

censored?

If how I choose to express myself, is censored?

If, I am censored?

The question lies not in my dignity or worth but in the

details which may be the same

What's the difference between

Strippers and burlesque?

Phone sex operators and a call center?

Sugar babies and a trophy wife?

If it's in the execution then talk to that man

that died on the cross, but I'm not like him.

I won't die for your sins

but I'll die for my motherfucking art.

Fuck Your Respectability Politics.

My art can't be censored.

Love Never Dies

|

Who was the first person to say, *love never dies*?

Bring them to me so I can look them in their eyes
and tell them to shut the fuck up

You see, my love died in 1995 and I haven't been
the same since.

It feels like I'm stuck in the same chapter
of some twisted book as I keep fighting,
clawing my way to death
just to be reunited with my love.

Imagine the purest form of love that could only survive throughout space and time ripped away with the blink of an eye.

Dead.

I have killed love more times than I've given love.

Completely decapitating love so that it has no chance of survival because if I fail again I may not survive.

Love doesn't die.

Understand that Love is an emotion and emotions are fleeting so they don't last and I should know because I'm emotional and then I become emotionless and then I'm a bitch.

to the same ol liars with the same ol rhetoric

who say, "I'd love you even though you have

depression and you're moody"

but it's funny how it often ends with

"I don't really want to deal with it anymore so I'm

just gonna leave you now. I'm not happy."

That love died.

So again I have to ask for someone

to bring the motherfucker to me

who said that, *love never dies*

because they have created this tainted toxic illusion

of what love is supposed to be.

They say that love is supposed to be unconditional

but every love has conditions.

I love you, until you hurt me, then I have to love myself more and I have to let you go.

So you see love dies.
It's sometimes slow, withering away like rose petals. Stiff and lifeless. Falling to the floor, becoming foot traffic's doormat. Crumbling to pieces like I have found myself so many times before.

When I've tried to make the pieces fit together that I reluctantly gave away.

You want a smile, here take this.
You want commitment, I'll commit to you.
You want me to trust you, here, you have my trust.
You want me to be vulnerable, I'll be that.

I'm passing out fragments of myself like luxuries to someone who couldn't afford it in the first place and I'm dying.

Literally, suffocating because I can feel her love die right along with me.

As I hear faint heartbeats.

Labored breathing.

My eyes slowly close and everything fades to black.

I find myself in this familiar dark place.

I'm rotting with the remains of past lovers.

My question wasn't rhetorical,

I'd really like to know the answer.

How did they come to this conclusion

because even in the afterlife

as I lay here inhaling the stench of my own

decomposing corpse.

I reminisce on my few triumphant attempts at love

and I can't deny that it existed.

It was real as I spoke abundance into her

and she spoke life into me.

It wasn't until I dug through the piles of bones,

found my most favorite lover and gently kissed

the forehead of her skull,

that I realized *love never dies*.

Behind the Poem

|

What ignited my ink?

|

Chaos Queen

|

I have never known peace. I was born into chaos
and pain, and those themes have followed me
throughout my life. Over time, I've realized that my
need for toxicity often stems from a craving for
passion.

|

Through therapy and self-reflection, I've become
self-aware enough to admit that I am flawed.
Sometimes, doing bad things feels good. Do I act
on those impulses? No, because I've learned to
recognize that they usually come from feeling
rejected, bored, or some other underlying emotion I
haven't yet addressed. I'm learning not to be
impulsive and to practice self-control

My Familiar

|

I love writing poems that are inspired by my paramours. There's something about those connections that makes the writing feel effortless, like we've done this before, like we're picking up right where we left off.

|

This particular poem stands out as one of the most natural love poems I've ever written—and honestly, it may be one of the most genuine ones I ever will.

It's the kind of piece that feels almost destined, as
if the emotions were already there, waiting to be
put into words.

Young Lady

|

This poem was inspired by an experience with this person that was so profoundly life changing and altered my perception of what control, submission and vulnerability really means to me.

|

Weight Room

|

I think there's something beautiful about giving someone your weight and them having the will and strength to carry it.

|

Chance

|

My love for Chance was cut short. This life was not meant for our love. I am sure in the next life, we will meet again. She is deceased now but I see her everyday.

|

Weeping Hollow

|

I wrote this out of frustration. Past partners have
often perceived me as cold and emotionless because I
do not cry. Since publishing my book in 2020, I
have shed very few tears. What once served as a
shield to protect me from those who hurt me has
now become something I fear may be a permanent
defect.

My sun is Cancer, my moon is Capricorn, and my
rising is Aquarius. I am deeply empathetic and
emotional—when I allow myself to be.

|

Lessons

I didn't grow up with a mother so I didn't learn a
lot of things about girlhood or womanhood. I
learned empathy and tolerance from my father, but
he couldn't teach me the lessons that I needed to
know to survive being a black woman. Every lesson
I learned, I learned the hard way, through trauma.
Life can be the greatest yet harshest teacher.

The Artist's Burden

My poetry is driven by the dark corners of my
mind. The emotions and thoughts I carry on a daily
basis make for good poems but not a healthy life.
This is the price I pay; I only hope it's enough for
me to survive.

The Most High

I wrote this poem to try to understand why
everything that I loved either refused to love me
back or would be the death of me. Why is my love
of choice broken, sad and high?

Undress in Black

|

This poem was my attempt to show what I look like
when I'm alone, when I don't have to perform or
wear a mask to make other people comfortable. It's
a vulnerable moment for me—asking myself, would
I still be loved if people saw how grotesque I feel
when the mechanisms I use to adorn myself are
stripped away?

|

It's a raw question, one that digs into the fear of
being truly seen for who I am underneath all the
layers I put on. I put a lot of pressure on myself to
be who I think my loved ones want me to be, but I
recently discovered that they do not need me to be
perfect. They really just want me to live.

Sad Mistress

|

My relationship with my depression is one of the
most important yet toxic relationships I have. At
times, it felt like I would die if I didn't feel that
heaviness. And when I did experience even a brief
moment of light or happiness, I was scared. It left
me feeling empty and hollow.

|

One of the harshest realities about happiness is that
it's fleeting—it never lasts because it's impossible to
be happy 100% of the time. For a long time,
holding on to my depression ensured

I wouldn't have to face the pain of having happiness taken away from me. But now, I'm learning to choose myself over everything else. I'm learning to cope with life's highs and lows, accepting that neither will last forever, and finding peace in that balance.

Functionally Depressed

|

I got tired of being strong, dependable, agreeable,

and being alone in my feelings. I was celebrated for

"having my shit together", but the truth was, I was

falling apart every day. I'd go to work, show up for

friends and family, but at the end of the night, I'd

pray I wouldn't see another sunrise.

I was doing everything I was supposed to do, yet I

felt incredibly sad and had no idea what to do with

that. I wrote this poem so that I could be

understood and maybe one day, my only

responsibility would be getting the help that I need.

|

APB

|

Have you ever looked at yourself in the mirror and
saw this dark, unfamiliar, distorted figure staring
back at you? Have you ever lost yourself?

|

Creation

|

Creation is a letter to myself , to say the things
that no one has ever told me before. It's on paper in
black and white, so... it must be true. Right?

|

Golds

|

I hoped to manifest this beautiful regal persona for
myself. Golds was a play on goals, which I very
vulnerably put onto paper. I am still working on
being golden.

|

Write Happy

My poetry is often sad, and I wanted to write something happy—something I felt wouldn't scare my audience away. But I no longer wish to write happy or pretty. I wish to write honestly, letting whatever words land on the paper be the words I am meant to feel.

Rituals

|

Love ties don't die easily. Looking back, I realize I didn't know how to be honest, vulnerable, or nurturing in that relationship, yet I couldn't bring myself to let them go. That experience taught me so much about the kind of person I want to be.

It really shaped my views on monogamy and dating, but I have to admit—the other person paid a heavy price for my growth. It's something I carry with me, a reminder of how much relationships can teach us, even when we're not at our best.

Patty's Trash

|

This is a story for another book. Patty's Trash is the
only poem that I regret putting in *I'm Happy*. I
thought that I was ready to speak my truth but
maybe this is a truth that is not worth exploring?

|

This poem has been removed from this book and
lives in the past, with the rest of my regrets

hap·pi·ness
/ˈhapēnəs/
noun

|

Happiness – a state of bliss. A kiss. A perfectly shaped tear. Happiness is family and acceptance, consistent wealth and prosperity. Happiness is truth.

Happiness is often found in a woman's essence, embrace, body, and aura. In a perfect world, happiness would mean having the presence of my mother and grandmother in this life with me.

Happiness is fleeting and elusive—often inconsistent and unreliable.

About the Author

Reneé Blackwell

Renee' Blackwell is a mental health advocate, dediated ghostwriter and published author celebrated for the evocative poetry collection, I'm Happy. With a deep-seated passion for writing, literacy, and storytelling, Renee' Blackwell crafts narratives that are whimsical, haunting, sad, dark, and beautiful, resonating deeply with readers. Renee'is a proud supporter of the LGBTQIA+ community, using their platform to champion inclusivity and understanding.

www.ingramcontent.com/pod-product-compliance
Lightning Source LLC
Chambersburg PA
CBHW051529120626
46551CB00012B/1148